# the BATHR⚾⚾M BASEBALL B⚾⚾K

By John Murphy

RED-LETTER PRESS, INC.
SADDLE RIVER, NEW JERSEY

# Introduction

It is only natural that our National Pastime be linked with another favorite pastime - reading in the bathroom.

Baseball arguably tops the interest level when it comes to trivia in the world of sports - and the questions compiled by John Murphy here are among the best anywhere. For added enjoyment, humorous quotes from the lavatory to the locker room pepper the pages in the form of "Relief Pitches."

A roll call to the following for their contributions: Geoff Scowcroft for his stirring rendition of *Casey at the Bath,* Glenn Fraller and Sylvia Martin for their typography, and Cyndi Bellerose for her artwork.

As for the author, Mr. Murphy is no Johnny-come-lately in the field of bathroom books. The scribe of the best-selling *Bathroom Sports Quiz Book,* and now *The Bathroom Baseball Book,* it can be safely said that, to the diehard bathroom reading sports fan, Murphy's books are #1 and #2.

Jack Kreismer
Publisher

# CASEY AT THE BATH

*(With apologies to Ernest Lawrence Thayer)*

Things looked grim for the Mudville Nine, the score was 4-2.
With men ahead of Casey, there was little they could do.
Then Flynn let drive a single and Blakey followed suit.
The crowd let loose a mighty roar; the opponents stood there
   mute.

"But where o' where is Casey?", the fans began to shout.
And in his place, up came Smith who made the final out.
There is no joy in Mudville - as you have supposed;
With Bathroom Baseball Book in hand, Mighty Casey's
   indisposed.

# The Bathroom Scale

*See how you rate on each of the baseball quizzes:*

| Score | Rating |
|-------|--------|
| 0-2 | Down the drain |
| 3-4 | Throw in the towel |
| 5-6 | Close shave |
| 7-8 | Razor-sharp |
| 9-10 | Royal Flush! |

1. Willie, Mickey and the Duke: For which team did each play his last Major League game?

2. Which left-handed pitcher has won the most games?

3. In December of 1971, the White Sox obtained the 1972 MVP from the Dodgers for Steve Huntz and a pitcher with nine years experience. Name the MVP and the pitcher. Hint: This hurler was still playing in 1988.

4. With what Major League team did Danny Ainge play?

5. What's the Major League record for hits in a game?

6. The starting first baseman for the Dodgers in their last game in Brooklyn later went on to hit 46 home runs in the 1961 season. Who is he?

7. Who's the only 300 game winner with only one 20 game winning season?

8. Name four of the six relievers who have won the Cy Young Award.

9. Walter Johnson's record of 3508 strikeouts lasted 56 years until 1983 when three pitchers passed it. Give all three.

10. Only four players with ten or more letters in their last names have hit 40 or more home runs in a season. Can you get two of them?

# 1      **Answers**

1. *Willie - the Mets; Mickey - the Yankees; Duke - the Giants.*

2. *Warren Spahn - 363.*

3. *The MVP was Richie Allen. The pitcher was Tommy John.*

4. *The Toronto Blue Jays, 1979-81. His lifetime batting average was .220.*

5. *Nine. Johnny Burnett of Cleveland went 9 for 11 in an 18 inning game in 1932.*

6. *Jim Gentile who had his big years with the Baltimore Orioles. Interestingly, Gil Hodges was the starting third baseman for the Dodgers that day.*

7. *Don Sutton.*

8. *Mike Marshall - Dodgers, 1974; Sparky Lyle - Yankees, 1977; Bruce Sutter - Cubs, 1979; Rollie Fingers - Brewers, 1981; Willie Hernandez - Tigers, 1984; and Steve Bedrosian - Phillies, 1987.*

9. *Nolan Ryan, Steve Carlton and Gaylord Perry.*

10. *Carl Yastrzemski, Ted Kluszewski, Roy Campanella and Rico Petrocelli.*

1. There have been six players who have played 22 or more seasons with only one team. Can you get four of them and their teams?

2. In 1978, Ozzie Smith played 159 games for the Padres, hit .258 and stole 40 bases. He finished second in the Rookie of the Year voting to a player who played only 89 games but tallied 23 homers. Who won the award?

3. Name the two Heisman Trophy winners who have been Major Leaguers.

4. Who holds the Major League consecutive game hitting streak record? How many games? What team stopped him?

5. What three brothers played the outfield together in a Major League game? With what team?

6. Who was the last pitcher to legally throw the spitter?

7. Name the infielders in the famous Abbott and Costello routine.

8. This player never led his league in home runs but has hit more All-Star Game homers than anyone else. Who is he?

9. Talking about home runs, what pitcher has the most career four-base hits (as a hurler)?

10. What two teams participated in the first World Series played entirely on artificial turf?

1. *Brooks Robinson, 23 years, Orioles; Carl Yastrzemski, 23, Red Sox; Cap Anson, 22, Cubs; Al Kaline, 22, Tigers; Stan Musial, 22, Cardinals; Mel Ott, 22, New York Giants.*

2. *Bob Horner of the Atlanta Braves.*

3. *Vic Janowicz and Bo Jackson.*

4. *Joe DiMaggio with 56 games. Cleveland stopped the streak.*

5. *Felipe, Matty and Jesus Alou with the San Francisco Giants.*

6. *Burleigh Grimes, whose last season was 1934.*

7. *First baseman - Who; second baseman - What; shortstop - I Don't Care; third baseman - I Don't Know.*

8. *Stan Musial. He has six All-Star home runs.*

9. *Wes Ferrell with 37.*

10. *The Philadelphia Phillies and the Kansas City Royals in 1980.*

---

### Relief Pitch

"It always did look like a toilet bowl. Now it has a seat on it."

    — *Whitey Herzog, about the new roof on Olympic Stadium in Montreal*

1. There have been five National League Rookies of the Year with only four letters in their last names. Can you think of three of them?

2. Who holds the career American League record for walking the most times? How about the National League?

3. Give the two managers in the 1951 Dodgers-Giants playoff.

4. Name the team that won a World Series before winning an Opening Day game.

5. What was the final score in the poem *Casey at the Bat?*

6. What's the call? A batter hits a ground ball past the pitcher but it hits the rubber and rolls into foul territory between first base and home.

7. Two pitchers have hit two World Series home runs. Name one of them.

8. What four teams won the World Series during the '50's?

9. In 1969, this Hall-of-Famer was intentially walked 45 times. Who is he?

10. How many consecutive games did Lou Gehrig play?

# 3          Answers

1.    *Alvin Dark, Willie Mays, Wally Moon, Pete Rose and Steve Howe.*

2.    *AL - Babe Ruth; NL - Joe Morgan.*

3.    *Giants - Leo Durocher; Dodgers - Chuck Dressen.*

4.    *New York Mets.*

5.    *4-2.*

6.    *Foul ball.*

7.    *Bob Gibson in 1967 and 1968; Dave McNally in 1969.*

8.    *New York Yankees - 1950, '51, '52, '53, '56, '58; New York Giants - 1954; Brooklyn/Los Angeles Dodgers - 1955, '59; Milwaukee Braves - 1957.*

9.    *Willie McCovey.*

10.   *2,130.*

## Relief Pitch

"It seems to me the official rule book should be called the funny pages. It obviously doesn't mean anything. The rule book is only good for you when you go deer hunting and run out of toilet paper."

— *Billy Martin, after particularly frequent run-ins with the umpires*

1.  Name the four men who have won consecutive Cy Young awards.

2.  Who is the oldest player to win a batting title?

3.  In 1983 and 1984 respectively, a Boston outfielder led the AL in both home runs and RBI's but did not win the MVP award. Can you recall these two Red Sox and the two players who did capture the MVP those years?

4.  Who was the youngest player elected to the Hall of Fame?

5.  Three Yankees have won the MVP award three times each. Name this talented trio.

6.  A St. Louis Brown player won Rookie of the Year and went on to hit 318 home runs in his career. Who is he?

7.  In 1987, four players joined the "30-30" club (i.e., hit 30 or more homers and stole 30 or more bases). This had happened only eleven times prior to that year. Can you name three of these four fleet-footed sluggers?

8.  What pitcher holds the record for the most shutouts in a season?

9.  True or False? Ty Cobb once led the Majors in home runs.

10. What catcher has won the most Gold Glove awards?

1.  Sandy Koufax, 1965 and '66; Denny McLain, 1968 and '69; Jim Palmer, 1975 and '76; Roger Clemens, 1986 and '87.

2.  Ted Williams - he was 39.

3.  In 1983, Jim Rice was beaten out by Cal Ripken, Jr. In 1984, Tony Armas - by Willie Hernandez.

4.  Sandy Koufax who was 35 when elected in 1971.

5.  Joe DiMaggio in 1939, '41 and '47; Yogi Berra in 1951, '54 and '55; Mickey Mantle in 1956, '57 and '62.

6.  Roy Sievers.

7.  Joe Carter, 31 HR - 31 SB; Eric Davis, 37 - 50; Howard Johnson, 36 -32; Darryl Strawberry, 39 - 34.

8.  Grover Cleveland Alexander who hurled 16 shutouts in 1916.

9.  True. In 1909, he led with 9 homers.

10. Johnny Bench.

1. There are eight players, whose names begin with the letter "M," who have hit more than 40 home runs in a season. Give six of them.

2. Who is the only player to have represented four different teams in All-Star Games?

3. Name the three brother combinations with the most combined wins.

4. In 1962, the All-Star MVP award was given for the first time. A Los Angeles player was named MVP in both All-Star games played that year. Can you recall the two recipients?

5. Who played Babe Ruth in the *Babe Ruth Story?*

6. This shortstop once hit 47 home runs in a season. Who is he?

7. What pitcher once struck out ten consecutive batters?

8. Who holds the AL record for RBI's in a season?

9. Name the three second basemen who have won the MVP award since 1950.

10. What Major League stadium currently has the largest seating capacity?

# 5       **Answers**

1.  *Mickey Mantle, Roger Maris, Eddie Mathews, Willie Mays, Willie McCovey, Mark McGwire, Johnny Mize and Dale Murphy.*

2.  *Goose Gossage. He represented the White Sox, Pirates, Yankees and Padres.*

3.  *373 wins - the Mathewsons: Christy (373), Henry (0); 529 wins - the Perrys: Gaylord (314), Jim (215). Phil and Joe Niekro, who passed the Perrys in 1987, are still adding to their total.*

4.  *Maury Wills of the Los Angeles Dodgers and Leon "Daddy Wags" Wagner of the Los Angeles Angels. (The Los Angeles Angels were renamed the California Angels in 1965.)*

5.  *William Bendix.*

6.  *Ernie Banks in 1958.*

7.  *Tom Seaver who struck out the last ten batters of a game against the San Diego Padres in 1970.*

8.  *Lou Gehrig who knocked in 184 runs in 1931.*

9.  *Nellie Fox, 1959; Joe Morgan, 1975 and '76; Ryne Sandburg, 1984.*

10.  *Cleveland Stadium which seats 74,208.*

1. List the six Major League stadiums named after people.

2. What team once won 26 straight games?

3. From 1942-44, three different Cardinals won the MVP award. Who were these three Redbirds?

4. This pitcher won 27 games for a last place club. Name him and his team.

5. These identical twins both played for Pittsburgh during the 50's. Each played the infield and pitched for the Pirates. Do you remember them?

6. With what team did Tom Seaver win his 300th game?

7. Who was the first player in the history of the San Diego Padres to have his uniform number retired?

8. Who was the youngest winner of an MVP award?

9. What player had the most hits in his last season?

10. True or False? In 1927, Babe Ruth hit more home runs in Yankee Stadium than on the road.

1.    *Comiskey Park, Wrigley Field, Shea Stadium, Busch Stadium, Jack Murphy Stadium, and the Hubert H. Humphrey Metrodome.*

2.    *The New York Giants in 1916. All 26 games were at home. (They finished fourth in the standings that year.)*

3.    *Mort Cooper, 1942; Stan Musial, 1943; Marty Marion, 1944.*

4.    *Steve Carlton of the Phillies in 1972.*

5.    *Eddie and Johnny O'Brien.*

6.    *The Chicago White Sox.*

7.    *Steve Garvey (#6), in 1988.*

8.    *Vida Blue. He turned 22 during the 1971 season when he won the award.*

9.    *Shoeless Joe Jackson - with 218 hits in 1920. He was banned from baseball after that year because of the Black Sox scandal.*

10.   *False. He hit 28 at Yankee Stadium and 32 on the road.*

### Relief Pitch

"Your body is just like a bar of soap. It gradually wears down from repeated use."

— *Richie Allen, nearing the end of his career*

1. With what team did Pete Rose get his 4,000th hit?

2. Despite the fact that these two players each won two MVP awards, they are not in the Hall of Fame - even though they are eligible for it. Name them both.

3. Name six of the seven Yankees who have won the Rookie of the Year award.

4. What two teams took part in the first night game in the Major Leagues?

5. What is the oldest Major League stadium still in use?

6. How many regular season home runs did Henry Aaron hit?

7. With what team did Ty Cobb get his 4,000th hit?

8. Who has the most career home runs for the Kansas City Royals?

9. This Boston pitcher won 17 games three straight years during the 1970's. Can you think of him?

10. Name the last National League team to win the World Series in consecutive years.

1.  *The Montreal Expos in 1984.*

2.  *Hal Newhouser who was the AL MVP in 1944 and '45; Roger Maris who duplicated this feat in 1960 and '61.*

3.  *Gil McDougald - 1951; Bob Grim - 1954; Tony Kubek -1957; Tom Tresh - 1962; Stan Bahnsen - 1968; Thurman Munson - 1970; Dave Righetti - 1981.*

4.  *The Cincinnati Reds beat the Philadelphia Phillies 2-1 at Crosley Field on May 24, 1935.*

5.  *Comiskey Park.*

6.  *755.*

7.  *The Philadelphia Athletics in 1927 (ironically, against the Tigers).*

8.  *George Brett.*

9.  *Bill Lee. In 1973, he was 17-11; in 1974, 17-15; in 1975, 17-9.*

10. *The Cincinnati Reds in 1975 and '76.*

1. Who are the six players to have won more than five batting titles apiece?

2. What is the middle name of the first black man to play in the Majors?

3. In what year was the World Series last played in one stadium and what teams were involved?

4. Name the Simon and Garfunkel song with the line, "Where have you gone, Joe DiMaggio?"

5. Who has hit the most Major League homers as a teenager?

6. Who holds the Major League record for grand slams in a season?

7. What pitcher holds the record for winning the most consecutive World Series games?

8. How many World Series did the Brooklyn Dodgers win?

9. It has happened only once that two brothers have pitched on the same team in both the American and National Leagues. Do you know them?

10. Who holds the Red Sox' consecutive game hitting streak record?

**8**     **Answers**

1.  *Ty Cobb, 12; Honus Wagner, 8; Rod Carew, 7; Stan Musial, 7; Rogers Hornsby, 7; Ted Williams, 6.*

2.  *Jack Roosevelt Robinson.*

3.  *1944. The St. Louis Cardinals and St. Louis Browns played all the games in Sportman's Park.*

4.  Mrs. Robinson.

5.  *Tony Conigliaro who hit 24 homers for the Red Sox before he turned 20.*

6.  *Don Mattingly who hit six in 1987.*

7.  *Bob Gibson - 7.*

8.  *One, in 1955.*

9.  *Phil and Joe Niekro. They pitched for the Atlanta Braves in 1973 and '74 and for the Yankees in 1985.*

10. *Dom DiMaggio, 34 in 1949.*

**Relief Pitch**

"We've got a problem. Luis Tiant wants to use the bathroom and it says no foreign objects in the toilet."
— *Graig Nettles, during a New York Yankees' airplane trip*

1.  Who is the only man to get 1,000 RBI's during the 1970's?

2.  Only two pitchers have struck out 4,000 batters, Who are they?

3.  About whom was Branch Rickey talking when he said, "He couldn't hit, couldn't run, couldn't field and couldn't throw, but was still the best player on the club. All he could do for you was win."?

4.  The National League added Houston and New York for the 1962 season. Name the managers of these expansion teams.

5.  How many World Series homers did Willie Mays hit?

6.  What National League clubs have won three straight World Series?

7.  Who pitched 12 perfect innings only to lose in the 13th? Do you recall the teams as well?

8.  Two American League rookies tossed no-hitters in 1973 - one for the Royals and one for the Rangers. Both pitchers' last names begin with the letter "B." Can you get them both?

9.  What was the original name of the Houston Astros?

10. What is a pitcher's E.R.A. if he gives up four earned runs in six innings?

# 9           Answers

1.  *Johnny Bench with 1,013.*

2.  *Nolan Ryan and Steve Carlton.*

3.  *Eddie Stanky.*

4.  *New York - Casey Stengel; Houston - Harry Craft.*

5.  *None (in 71 at-bats).*

6.  *No National League club has ever won three straight World Series.*

7.  *Harvey Haddix of the Pirates who lost to the Braves 1-0.*

8.  *Steve Busby of the Royals and Jim Bibby of the Rangers.*

9.  *Houston Colt 45's.*

10. *6.00.*

1. There have been two players elected to the Hall of Fame less than a year after playing their last game. Can you think of them?

2. What was the last American League club to win three straight World Series?

3. In the 1956 World Series, in games three through seven, five different Yankee pitchers threw complete games. Give three of them.

4. In which World Series was the first game played within a domed stadium?

5. What baseball player's wife is a member of the LPGA Hall of Fame?

6. Of all the players whose names begin with the letter "I," this player has the most home runs. Who is he?

7. True or False? The Milwaukee Brewers finished last in the American League in 1901.

8. Who was the first native Puerto Rican to win 20 games in a season?

9. These two players each player 24 All Star Games. Give both of them.

10. Who holds the rookie record for home runs in a season?

1.  *Lou Gehrig in 1939 and Roberto Clemente in 1973.*

2.  *The Oakland A's, 1972-74.*

3.  *In order: Whitey Ford, Tom Sturdivant, Don Larsen, Bob Turley and Johnny Kucks.*

4.  *1987 - The St. Louis Cardinals at the Minnesota Twins.*

5.  *Ray Knight who is married to Nancy Lopez.*

6.  *Monte Irvin with 99.*

7.  *True. The next year they moved to St. Louis and became the Browns. Eventually, the Browns moved to Baltimore where they became the Orioles.*

8.  *Ed Figueroa in 1978 when he was 20-9.*

9.  *Stan Musial and Willie Mays.*

10. *Mark McGwire who hit 49 in 1987.*

## Relief Pitch

"They move very, very reluctantly. I think it was a long time before any of them had inside plumbing."

— *Baltimore Orioles owner Edward Bennett Williams,*
*discussing the conservative National League owners*

1.  On August 4, 1985, a pitcher won his 300th game on the East Coast and a batter got his 3,000th hit on the West Coast. Name these two players.

2.  Who is the only manager to win the World Series in his first two years?

3.  What teams did Yogi Berra play for?

4.  What player pitched exactly five games for a team over a fourteen-year period and won all of them?

5.  These two pitchers, who played in the Majors during the 50's and 60's, later became Congressmen. Do you recall them?

6.  In a game in 1962, Roger Maris was intentionally walked four times. How many intentional passes did he receive in 1961 when he hit 61 homers?

7.  Who are the only two managers to win at least 600 games with two different teams? Name all four clubs as well.

8.  Is it legal to hit a pitch that bounces before the plate?

9.  Which team always has its Opening Day game at home and why?

10. In the annals of Major League ball, only one man has played with the initials "T.Z." Who?

# 11    Answers

1.  Tom Seaver and Rod Carew.

2.  Ralph Houk with the 1961 and '62 Yankees.

3.  The Yankees and Mets.

4.  Babe Ruth. In 1920, he was 1-0; 1921, 2-0; 1930, 1-0; 1933, 1-0. These were the only games that he pitched for the Yankees.

5.  Wilmer "Vinegar Bend" Mizell who pitched for the Cardinals, Pirates and Mets and Jim Bunning of the Tigers, Phillies, Pirates and Dodgers.

6.  None.

7.  Sparky Anderson with the Reds and Tigers; Leo Durocher with the Dodgers and Giants.

8.  Yes.

9.  The Cincinnati Reds. The reason is to honor them as the first professional baseball team.

10. Tom Zachary who pitched from 1918-1936 and is best known for giving up Babe Ruth's 60th home run in 1927. Curiously, although he played with the name Tom, his real first name was Jonathan.

1. Name the two brothers who won all four games of a World Series.

2. What Hall-of-Famer hit home runs to win the only two games that the Giants won in the 1923 Series against the Yankees.

3. In 1974, Henry Aaron hit home run number 715 to break Babe Ruth's record. Against what team did he hit this record-shattering blast? Who was the pitcher? What was the uniform number of the pitcher?

4. Who is the only man to strike out 200 or more batters for nine straight years?

5. What is your slugging percentage for the day if you get up five times, hitting two singles and a double and striking out twice?

6. The *Baseball Encyclopedia* lists two nicknames for Joe Dimaggio. What are they?

7. What manager has the most wins?

8. In 1905, this pitcher threw three shutouts in the World Series. Who is he?

9. Who was the first black pitcher in each league to win a World Series game?

10. Only one player whose last name starts with the letter "Y" has hit more than 450 homers in his career. Spell his last name.

1. *Dizzy and Paul "Daffy" Dean. They each won two games in the 1934 Series for the Cardinals against the Tigers.*

2. *Casey Stengel.*

3. *Aaron hit the homer off Al Downing of the Los Angeles Dodgers. Both pitcher and hitter wore uniform number 44.*

4. *Tom Seaver.*

5. *.800.*

6. *"Joltin' Joe" and "The Yankee Clipper."*

7. *Connie Mack (a.k.a. Cornelius McGillicuddy).*

8. *Christy Mathewson of the New York Giants against the Philadelphia Athletics.*

9. *National League - Joe Black of the Brooklyn Dodgers in 1952; American League - Jim "Mudcat" Grant of the Minnesota Twins in 1965.*

10. *Y-a-s-t-r-z-e-m-s-k-i.*

## Relief Pitch

"His only weakness is he's gotta shave twice a day."
— Chuck Tanner, *speaking about prospect Rick Reichardt in 1964*

1. What three switch-hitters have the most career home runs?

2. Who struck out 20 batters in a nine-inning game? Who fanned more than twenty in a game?

3. This Hall-of-Famer pitched a perfect game and, in that game, had three hits and three RBI's. Who is he and what is his real first name?

4. How many of the bases are in fair territory?

5. Only once in the last 50 years has a pitcher won the last game of the World Series two years in a row. Can you name this Yankee?

6. On May 1, 1920, Leon Cadore of the Brooklyn Dodgers and Joe Oeschger of the Boston Braves each hurled a complete game against one another. The result was a 1-1 tie. What was even more remarkable about this game?

7. Who is the only man to have hit 40 or more home runs in a season in each league?

8. Name the three teams which have drawn three million fans at home in a season.

9. Give one of the two Major League teams that the *Rifleman* - Chuck Connors - played for. Do you know his position?

10. Who is the youngest person to have ever played in the Majors?

1. *Mickey Mantle, Reggie Smith and Eddie Murray.*

2. *Roger Clemens of the Red Sox had 20 strikeouts in a nine-inning contest in 1986; Tom Cheney of the Washington Senators whiffed 21 in sixteen innings in 1962.*

3. *James "Catfish" Hunter who managed this feat against the Twins in 1968.*

4. *All four.*

5. *Allie Reynolds in 1952-53 versus the Dodgers.*

6. *It went 26 innings.*

7. *Darrell Evans. He did it for the Braves in 1973 and the Tigers in 1985.*

8. *Los Angeles Dodgers, New York Mets and St. Louis Cardinals.*

9. *He played first base with the Brooklyn Dodgers and the Chicago Cubs.*

10. *Joe Nuxhall of the Reds who was 15 years, 10 months and 11 days old when he made his debut in 1944.*

1. What person was Warren Spahn referring to when he said that he played for him both before and after he was a genius?

2. The 1986 Tigers had six players hit 20 or more homers. Can you name five of them?

3. Only one player in the last 50 years has gotten pinch hits from both sides of the plate in the same World Series. Who is this singular switch-hitter? Hint: He did it in 1986.

4. In 1961, these two Tigers drove in more than 130 runs apiece. Who are they?

5. What pitcher has walked the most batters in his career?

6. Name the two men who hit home runs in eight consecutive games.

7. Who was the first President of the United States to watch a Major League game while in office?

8. Who played his entire fifteen-year career with the Minnesota Twins?

9. A line drive hits the second base umpire on a fly and ricochets to the shortstop who catches it before it hits the ground. The shortstop throws to first too late to get the batter. Is the batter out, safe, or does it count as a foul ball?

10. True or False? When he was a child, George Steinbrenner was a Yankee batboy.

1.  *Casey Stengel. Spahn played for him on the '42 Braves and the '65 Mets.*

2.  *Darrell Evans, 29; Kirk Gibson, 28; Lance Parrish, 22; Alan Trammell, 21; Darnell Coles, 20; Lou Whitaker, 20.*

3.  *Lee Mazzilli of the Mets.*

4.  *Norm Cash and Rocky Colavito.*

5.  *Nolan Ryan.*

6.  *Dale Long and Don Mattingly.*

7.  *Benjamin Harrison in 1892.*

8.  *Tony Oliva.*

9.  *He's safe (assuming that the umpire is in fair territory). The umps are considered part of the field.*

10. *False. Ol' George started at the top.*

## Relief Pitch

"It's like playing with marbles in a bathtub."
— *Chicago White Sox pitcher Dave Lemonds, on the new artificial turf in Kansas City in 1973*

1. Name one of the three pitchers who faced the Braves while they were in Boston, Milwaukee and Atlanta.

2. What San Diego pitcher lost 20 games in 1974 and won 20 the next year?

3. In its second year of existence, this expansion team had the third best record in the league. Do you recall the team and the manager? Hint: The year was 1962.

4. The 1910 Philadelphia Athletics used only two pitchers in defeating the Cubs 4-1 in the World Series. Name one of these hurlers.

5. During the 60's, two National Leaguers hit World Series grand slams. Can you get either one?

6. What team within the past 80 years won 217 regular season games within a two-year period?

7. In 1975, this Hall-of-Famer batted .201 in 482 at-bats. Who is he?

8. Who has exactly 3,000 career hits?

9. Name the only man to hit five home runs in a World Series.

10. The closest MVP tally ever was decided by one vote. Who beat whom? Hint: The loser won the Triple Crown that year.

# 15    Answers

1.  *Robin Roberts, Curt Simmons and Hoyt Wilhelm.*

2.  *Randy Jones.*

3.  *The Los Angeles Angels managed by Bill Rigney.*

4.  *Jack Coombs who was 3-0 and Chief Bender who was 1-1.*

5.  *Chuck Hiller of the Giants in 1962 and Ken Boyer of the Cardinals in 1964. Hiller's blast was the first World Series grand slam ever by a NL player.*

6.  *The 1969-70 Baltimore Orioles.*

7.  *Brooks Robinson.*

8.  *Roberto Clemente.*

9.  *Reggie Jackson in 1977.*

10. *In 1947, Joe DiMaggio edged Ted Williams by a mere vote.*

1.  Name the three men whose last names begin with the letter "S" who have more than 400 career homers.

2.  In 1959, the top two American League hitters were Tigers and had the same first letter in their last names. Give them both.

3.  This Hall-of-Famer has walked the most batters in a season. Who is he?

4.  Name one of the two pitchers to win 40 games in a single year.

5.  If a bunted ball rolls and stops right on the foul line between third and home, is it fair or foul?

6.  Only two catchers have ever led their leagues in triples. Name one of them. Hint: Both played during the 1980's.

7.  Four players since 1940 have driven in more than 150 runs in a season. Can you remember two of them?

8.  Who holds the Chicago White Sox record for career home runs?

9.  The Yankees won five consecutive pennants twice. In what years?

10. Give the three rivers for which Three Rivers Stadium is named.

1.    *Mike Schmidt, Willie Stargell and Duke Snider.*

2.    *Harvey Kuenn who battted .353 and Al Kaline with .327.*

3.    *Bob Feller who walked 208 batters in 1938. He none-theless managed a record of 17-11.*

4.    *Jack Chesbro who won 41 in 1904 and Ed Walsh who had 40 victories in 1908.*

5.    *Fair. The foul lines, like the foul poles, are in fair territory.*

6.    *Tim McCarver led the NL in 1966 and Carlton Fisk tied for the AL lead in 1972. By the way, McCarver had five at-bats in the 80's with one hit.*

7.    *Ted Williams and Vern Stephens of the Red Sox each drove in 159 runs in 1949; Joe DiMaggio of the Yankees, 155 in 1948; Tommy Davis of the Dodgers, 153 in 1962.*

8.    *Harold Baines.*

9.    *1949-53 and 1960-64.*

10.   *The Ohio, Allegheny and Monongahela.*

1.  Two years before pitching a perfect game, this hurler was 3-21 for the Orioles. Four years later, he was 1-10 for the A's. Who is he?

2.  The 1986 World Champion New York Mets had two pitchers on their staff who were Hawaiian born. Can you name them both?

3.  The only home run champion to have failed to ever drive in 100 runs was a Chicago White Sox infielder. Who?

4.  What three pitchers won the most games in relief?

5.  This Hall-of-Famer lost the first World Series game. Do you know him?

6.  Name the movie made about Lou Gehrig. What Oscar-winning actor portrayed the "Iron Man"?

7.  In the same movie, what big leaguer played Gehrig in the long-distance batting sequences? Hint: This lifetime .324 hitter is the only man to hit for the cycle twice in a season.

8.  Which pitcher had the best season E.R.A. in the past 60 years?

9.  This Hall-of-Famer, who retired in 1974, ended his career with 399 regular season home runs. Can you name him?

10. Who is the only manager to have won a World Series in each league?

**17**     **Answers**

1.   *Don Larsen.*

2.   *Ron Darling and Sid Fernandez.*

3.   *Bill Melton who led the AL with 33 HR's in 1971. His best RBI output was 96 in 1970.*

4.   *Hoyt Wilhelm - 123; Lindy McDaniel - 119; and Rollie Fingers - 107.*

5.   *Cy Young.*

6.   Pride of the Yankees. *Gary Cooper played Gehrig.*

7.   *Babe Herman.*

8.   *Bob Gibson with a 1.12 E.R.A. in 1968.*

9.   *Al Kaline.*

10.  *Sparky Anderson with the Reds in 1975 and '76, and with the Tigers in 1984.*

1.  In 1927, these two brothers combined for 460 hits. Can you come up with this pair and the team on which they played?

2.  What shortstop has the most career home runs?

3.  Which team has retired the most numbers?

4.  The 1982 Milwaukee Brewers had three players get 200 or more hits. Name all three.

5.  Who are the three 3,000 hit players with lifetime averages of less than .300?

6.  From 1962-66, this pitcher (who threw a perfect game) won 19 games four different times. Who is he?

7.  Is it possible for a pitcher to throw a perfect game and yet have his team make an error during the game?

8.  What was the final score of the only perfect game in World Series history?

9.  Who holds the Major League record for RBI's in a season and what is it?

10. In the last 50 years, only three men have pitched more than 350 innings in a season. Name one of them.

1.   *Paul and Lloyd Waner of the Pirates.*

2.   *Ernie Banks - 293.*

3.   *The New York Yankees.*

4.   *Robin Yount - 210; Cecil Cooper - 205; Paul Molitor -201.*

5.   *Lou Brock - .293; Al Kaline - .297; Carl Yastrzemski -.285.*

6.   *Jim Bunning.*

7.   *Yes, if the error is on a foul pop.*

8.   *2-0.*

9.   *Hack Wilson of the Cubs who got 190 in 1930.*

10.  *Wilbur Wood of the White Sox who had 377 in 1972 and 359 in 1973; Mickey Lolich of the Tigers, 376 in 1971; and Bob Feller of the Indians, 371 in 1946.*

## Relief Pitch

"I flush the john between innings to keep my wrists strong."

— *Designated hitter John Lowenstein, on how he stays ready while on the bench*

1. There have been five players with more than 400 home runs who have pitched in the Majors. How many can you get?

2. What animal did Bill Lee say that Don Zimmer resembled?

3. For two consecutive years, a team managed by Alfred beat a team skippered by Dorrel in the American League Championship Series. By what names are these two more commonly known?

4. Who is the youngest man to be an Opening Day pitcher within the last 50 years?

5. In 1985, a Cincinnati rookie won 20 games. Do you recall him?

6. Name one of the two current NL teams that have not had a Rookie of the Year.

7. True or False? At one time in the Major Leagues, if a fair ball bounced into the outfield stands between the foul poles, it was a home run.

8. What Dodger pitcher has the most victories?

9. Name the only two black pitchers to strike out 300 or more batters in a season.

10. Since it first started in 1903, the World Series was not held in what year?

1. *Babe Ruth, Jimmie Foxx, Ted Williams, Stan Musial and Dave Kingman.*

2. *A gerbil.*

3. *Billy Martin and Whitey Herzog. Martin's Yankees downed Herzog's Royals in 1976 and '77.*

4. *Dwight Gooden who was 20 years, 4 months and 24 days old.*

5. *Tom Browning with a record of 20-9.*

6. *Pittsburgh Pirates and Houston Astros.*

7. *True. The rule was changed in 1931. By the way, none of Ruth's 60 homers in 1927 bounced into the stands.*

8. *Don Sutton.*

9. *J. R. Richard with 303 in 1978 and 313 in 1979; Vida Blue with 301 in 1971.*

10. *1904. John McGraw's New York Giants disdained to play the upstart Boston team.*

1. Which four pitchers have won the most Major League games?

2. Two hurlers have won exactly 300 games. Who are they?

3. Give the real first names of these two 300 game winners.

4. The 1958 and '59 AL Rookies of the Year both played for Washington. Do you know them?

5. What member of the Baseball Hall of Fame once played basketball for the Harlem Globetrotters?

6. Combined, how many homers did Mantle and Maris hit in 1961?

7. Who won his 300th game with the Seattle Mariners?

8. In what ballpark was the Beatles last concert held?

9. Name the only brother battery in an All-Star Game.

10. Who are the four men to hit safely in 40 straight games in this century?

1.  *Cy Young - 511; Walter Johnson - 416; Grover Cleveland Alexander - 373; Christy Mathewson - 373.*

2.  *Lefty Grove and Early Wynn.*

3.  *Robert Moses (Grove) and Early (Wynn).*

4.  *1958 - Albie Pearson; 1959 - Bob Allison.*

5.  *Bob Gibson.*

6.  *115.*

7.  *Gaylord Perry.*

8.  *Candlestick Park.*

9.  *Mort and Walker Cooper in 1942.*

10. *Joe DiMaggio - 56 in 1941; Pete Rose - 44 in 1978; George Sisler - 41 in 1922; Ty Cobb - 40 in 1911.*

## Relief Pitch

"They all changed. Most of them got agents, and I ceased to talk to 'em. 'Like to use the toilet paper?' 'Dunno, I gotta talk to my agent.'"

> — *Former pitcher and forever flake, Bill Lee, on today's players*

1. In 1936, the Hall of Fame was opened and five men were enshrined. Name these early superstars.

2. Only one of these five charter members of the Hall of Fame never managed. Who?

3. Which member of this quintet played for only one team during his career?

4. Name the four Pirates who have won MVP awards within the past 50 years.

5. Of all the pitchers who have thrown no-hitters, who has the shortest surname? Hint: He was born in France and played for the Expos.

6. What two men have the most multiple-home run games in Major League history?

7. What person has received the most votes for the All-Star team during his career?

8. Who holds the NL record for home runs in a season?

9. What Hall of Fame pitcher has won more World Series games than anyone else? What pitcher has lost the most?

10. True or False? Vince DiMaggio hit more grand slams in his career than his brother, Joe, did.

1. *Babe Ruth, Ty Cobb, Honus Wagner, Christy Mathewson and Walter Johnson.*

2. *Babe Ruth, although Wagner only managed five games.*

3. *Walter Johnson. Christy Mathewson almost made it. He played 636 games - 635 for the New York Giants and one for the Cincinnati Reds.*

4. *Dick Groat, 1960; Roberto Clemente, 1966; Dave Parker, 1978; Willie Stargell, 1979.*

5. *Charlie Lea.*

6. *Babe Ruth with 72 and Willie Mays with 63.*

7. *Rod Carew with more than 33 million.*

8. *Hack Wilson had 56 in 1930.*

9. *Whitey Ford was 10-8. Both are World Series records.*

10. *False, although in their most productive years for grand slams, Vince hit four (for the Phillies in 1945) and Joe "only" hit three (with the Yanks in 1937).*

1. List four of the five men who threw two no-hitters in the same year.

2. Sandy Koufax and Juan Marichal were two of the top pitchers of the '60's. With what teams did they end their careers?

3. Who is the only man to lead the Major Leagues in strikeouts and E.R.A., yet still have a losing record that season?

4. The last brother battery occurred in the late '50's and early 60's. Can you name these siblings?

5. In 1969, the fans from each Major League city picked their all-time All-Star team. The Red Sox and Indians' fans agreed on a center fielder. Who was it?

6. Who was the youngest player to reach 100 career home runs?

7. Who is the only Cy Young award winner to have a son play in the Majors?

8. Give the real first and middle names of Casey Stengel. Why was he called "Casey"?

9. Which one of these three Hall-of-Famers did not have 100 career home runs: Home Run Baker, Ty Cobb, or Honus Wagner?

10. What catcher caught two of Sandy Koufax's no-hitters?

1. *Johnny Vander Meer in 1938; Allie Reynolds in 1951; Virgil Trucks in 1952; Jim Maloney in 1965; Nolan Ryan in 1973. Vander Meer's no-hitters were consecutive. Maloney lost his first one 1-0 by giving up a hit in the tenth inning.*

2. *Both ended their careers with the Dodgers.*

3. *Nolan Ryan in 1987. He went 8-16 for Houston.*

4. *Norm and Larry Sherry who played together from 1959-62 with the Los Angeles Dodgers.*

5. *Tris Speaker.*

6. *Tony Conigliaro.*

7. *Vernon Law.*

8. *Charles Dillon Stengel. He was called "Casey" because he was born in Kansas City.*

9. *Home Run Baker - he had 96. Cobb had 118 and Wagner, 101.*

10. *John Roseboro.*

## Relief Pitch

"Rube Waddell . . . loved pitching, fishing and drinking. When he died, they found him in a gin-filled bathtub with three drunken trout."

— *Mike Royko*, Chicago Sun-Times

1. Phil Roof and two other players are the only men to have played for the Milwaukee Braves and Brewers. Who are the other two? Hint: Each led the Majors in hits twice.

2. Name the Dodger losing pitchers in the 1951 Dodger-Giant playoff.

3. Who is the only man in the last 50 years to pitch a no-hitter and later manage a World Series winner?

4. True or False? When they started in 1961, the Angels played their home games at Wrigley Field.

5. What two teams participated in the first World Series night game?

6. First and second, one out. The batter hits a slow grounder to third. The third baseman picks up the ball with his bare hand and dives toward the bag. He touches the base with his empty glove just before the runner does. Is the runner out or safe?

7. What man managed for fifty years? Which team?

8. Who has hit the most lead-off homers?

9. This Hall of Fame pitcher batted .433 with 42 hits and knocked in 20 runs while winning 20 games that season. Who is he?

10. There has been a tie in the Cy Young voting only once. Do you recall the co-winners?

1.  *Felipe Alou and Henry Aaron.*

2.  *Ralph Branca lost them both - the first as a starter, the second in relief.*

3.  *Bob Lemon. He pitched a no-hitter in 1948 and led the 1978 Yankees to the World Championship.*

4.  *True. They used Wrigley Field in Los Angeles which was owned by the Wrigley family of Chicago and previously used for the Cubs' minor league team.*

5.  *On October 13, 1971, the Pirates beat the Orioles 4-3 at Pittsburgh in the first World Series night game.*

6.  *He's out. Since it's a force play, the fielder may touch the base with any part of his body.*

7.  *Connie Mack - The Philadelphia Athletics. He also managed the Pittsburgh Pirates from 1894-96.*

8.  *Rickey Henderson.*

9.  *Walter Johnson in 1925.*

10. *In 1969, Mike Cuellar of the Orioles and Denny McLain of the Tigers shared the honor.*

1.  Four members of the Boston Red Sox knocked in 100 or more runs in 1977. Who are they?

2.  Who was the first black pitcher to appear in a World Series game?

3.  Who was the first baseball player to earn $100,000 per year?

4.  Name the four positions at which Pete Rose played over 600 games.

5.  Of all the players who have had their numbers retired, which number is the largest?

6.  Only once has there been a tie in the MVP voting. What two first basemen were co-winners of the award?

7.  A rookie has gotten 200 or more hits only sixteen times. In 1964, both Rookies of the Year achieved this distinction. Name them.

8.  On March 15, 1978, the San Francisco Giants traded Gary Alexander, Gary Thomasson, Dave Heaverlo, Alan Wirth, John Henry Johnson, Phil Huffman, Mario Guerrero and $390,000 for one player. Who?

9.  Who won the Cy Young Award with the fewest victories? How many?

10. What's the rule in the Houston Astrodome if a fly ball hits the ceiling or one of the speakers suspended from it?

1. *Jim Rice - 114; Butch Hobson - 112; Carlton Fisk - 102; Carl Yastrzemski - 102.*

2. *Satchel Paige who appeared for Cleveland in game five of the 1948 Series against the Boston Braves.*

3. *Joe DiMaggio in 1949.*

4. *Outfield - 1327; first base - 939; third base - 634; second base - 628.*

5. *Don Drysdale's number 53.*

6. *Keith Hernandez of the Cardinals and Willie Stargell of the Pirates shared the MVP in 1979.*

7. *Tony Oliva of the Twins got 217 hits and Richie Allen of the Phillies tallied 201.*

8. *Vida Blue of Oakland. The other players all went on to the Majors.*

9. *Steve Bedrosian of the Phillies. He won five games.*

10. *The ball is in play. If it is caught on a fly, the batter is out.*

## Relief Pitch

"Lopat looks like he is throwing wads of tissue paper. Every time he wins a game, fans come down out of the stands asking for contracts."

— *Casey Stengel, discussing Yankee pitcher Eddie Lopat's slow stuff*

1. Three shortstops have won NL batting titles. All three men played for the Pittsburgh Pirates. Can you list them?

2. Who holds the National League record for consecutive games played?

3. Name the three men with the most home runs who are not in the Hall of Fame.

4. Who won the first Cy Young Award?

5. Only once in an All-Star Game have there been co-winners of the MVP award. This happened in 1975 when two players with similar sounding names tied. Who are these National Leaguers?

6. In the 1981 strike-shortened season, eight teams made it into post-season play. Can you think of all eight?

7. Who hit the first home run in Yankee Stadium?

8. What three NL clubs are the only ones to have finished in tenth place?

9. Cy Young threw three Opening Day shutouts. The only other pitcher to do this played for the Phillies in the '50's, '60's and '70's. Who is he?

10. When was the last World Series sweep?

1.   *Honus Wagner in 1900, '03, '04, '06, '07, '08, '09 and '11; Arky Vaughn in 1935; and Dick Groat in 1960.*

2.   *Steve Garvey.*

3.   *Mike Schmidt, Reggie Jackson and Dave Kingman.*

4.   *Don Newcombe in 1956.*

5.   *Bill Madlock of the Cubs and Jon Matlack of the Mets.*

6.   *Montreal Expos, Philadelphia Phillies, Los Angeles Dodgers, Houston Astros, New York Yankees, Milwaukee Brewers, Oakland A's, Kansas City Royals.*

7.   *Babe Ruth in 1923.*

8.   *New York Mets - 1962, '63, '64, '65, '67; Chicago Cubs - 1966; Houston Astros - 1968.*

9.   *Chris Short.*

10.  *1976 - Cincinnati Reds over the New York Yankees.*

1. Three men have hit more than 40 homers and then managed World Series winners. Can you get two out of three?

2. What Hall-of-Famer struck out fifteen batters in his first big league appearance?

3. Which World Series ended with a home run? Who hit it?

4. Name the two Cleveland Indians who have won MVP awards in the past 50 years.

5. What team did midget Eddie Gaedel play for? Give his career Major League statistics.

6. Name the last two pitchers to shut out the opposition in the seventh game of the World Series.

7. Who is the oldest pitcher to strike out 300 men in a season?

8. In 1972, this Montreal hurler threw the first Major League no-hitter outside of the United States. Who is he?

9. Since 1970, three clubs have gone 108-54 in a season. Can you think of two of them?

10. This 1950 MVP led the Major Leagues in sacrifices four consecutive years. Name him.

1. *Davy Johnson who hit 43 homers in 1973 and managed the 1986 Mets; Gil Hodges, 42 in 1954 - he managed the 1969 Mets; Rogers Hornsby who hit 42 in 1922 and managed the 1926 Cardinals.*

2. *Bob Feller.*

3. *The 1960 Series. It ended when Pittsburgh's Bill Mazeroski hit a leadoff home run in the ninth to beat the Yankees 10-9 in the game and 4-3 in the series.*

4. *Lou Boudreau in 1948 and Al Rosen in 1953.*

5. *The St. Louis Browns. In 1951, he played one game and walked in his only plate appearance.*

6. *Bret Saberhagen of the Royals shut out the Cardinals 11-0 in 1985; Sandy Koufax of the Dodgers blanked the Twins 2-0 in 1965.*

7. *Mike Scott of the Astros in 1986. He was 31 when he struck out 306 batters.*

8. *Bill Stoneman.*

9. *The 1970 Baltimore Orioles; the 1975 Cincinnati Reds; and the 1986 New York Mets.*

10. *Phil Rizzuto.*

1. Which four Major League stadiums are named after the counties in which they are located?

2. What team lost the most games in a season?

3. Name the two managers who have won 10 pennants apiece.

4. Who is the only 40-year-old to win the Cy Young Award?

5. From 1979 to 1982, only Dodgers won the National League Rookie of the Year awards. Can you think of all four players?

6. Who is the first baseman that Lou Gehrig replaced?

7. Can you come up with a player with both a pitching percentage of 1.000 and more than 500 home runs?

8. They started giving World Series MVP awards in 1955. The first five winners were all pitchers. How many can you get?

9. What's the most home runs hit in a season by a player who did not win the HR title that year. Who did it?

10. Who was the first Yankee to win the AL home run championship?

1. *The A's play in Oakland-Alameda County Stadium; the Braves, Fulton County Stadium; the Brewers, Milwaukee County Stadium; the Mariners, the Kingdome.*

2. *The 1962 New York Mets - they lost 120.*

3. *John McGraw and Casey Stengel.*

4. *Gaylord Perry who did it in 1978 when he pitched for San Diego.*

5. *Rick Sutcliffe, 1979; Steve Howe, 1980; Fernando Valenzuela, 1981; and Steve Sax, 1982.*

6. *Wally Pipp.*

7. *Slugger Jimmie Foxx pitched one game for the Red Sox in 1939 and nine games for the Phillies in 1945. He wound up 1-0.*

8. *Johnny Podres, 1955; Don Larsen, 1956; Lew Burdette, 1957; Bob Turley, 1958; Larry Sherry, 1959.*

9. *Mickey Mantle's 54 in 1961.*

10. *Wally Pipp - he led in 1916 and '17.*

## Relief Pitch

"Nowadays they have more trouble packing hair dryers than baseball equipment."

     — *Bob Lemon, on ballplayers drying their "doo" in front of the bathroom mirror*

1.  With two outs and trailing by a run in the bottom of the ninth inning of the seventh game of the World Series, this player tried to steal second and was thrown out to end the game and the Series. Who was this base runner?

2.  What stadiums have been used for both a World Series and a Super Bowl?

3.  What pitchers gave up Roger Maris' 60th and 61st home runs?

4.  The Triple Crown has been won five times in the last 50 years. Who are the four American Leaguers to have done it?

5.  Who is the only player to get five hits in a World Series game?

6.  Mickey Mantle is one of only four men to have won the MVP and have double initials (in his case, "MM"). Can you get the other three?

7.  In 1977, two Minnesota teammates finished one-two in hitting in the AL. Within two years, both had played for California. Identify this duo.

8.  Name the pitcher, batter and fielder who made the last out in the 1962 World Series. What was the final score of the game?

9.  In 1969, what expansion teams entered the Majors?

10. Only three Detroit Tigers have ever hit *more* than 40 homers in a season. Give all of them.

1.  *Babe Ruth who did this in the 1926 Series against the Cardinals.*

2.  *San Diego's Jack Murphy Stadium and the Los Angeles Coliseum.*

3.  *60th - Jack Fisher of the Orioles; 61st - Tracy Stallard of the Red Sox.*

4.  *Ted Williams, 1942 and '47; Mickey Mantle, 1956; Frank Robinson, 1966; Carl Yastrzemski, 1967.*

5.  *Paul Molitor in game one of the 1982 World Series.*

6.  *Dizzy Dean in 1934; Marty Marion in 1944; and Jackie Jensen in 1958.*

7.  *Rod Carew and Lyman Bostock.*

8.  *Bobby Richardson caught a line drive off the bat of San Francisco's Willie McCovey. Ralph Terry pitched a 1-0 shutout for the Yankees.*

9.  *Kansas City Royals, Seattle Pilots, Montreal Expos and San Diego Padres.*

10. *Hank Greenberg, Rocky Colavito and Norm Cash.*

1. What three members of the Hall of Fame played during the 1970's and never spent a day in the minor leagues?

2. What Cuban pitcher once struck out 19 men in a Major League game?

3. Name the six big league teams that Dick Williams has managed.

4. Including the current one, list the last three Dodger managers.

5. Only three American League teams have ever finished in tenth place in the standings. Give all three.

6. Who are the two youngest Cy Young Award winners?

7. In 1986, this pitcher set a record by striking out the first seven batters in a game. In another game that same year, he threw a no-hitter - although he walked seven. Who is he?

8. Alphabetically, what baseball manager comes last?

9. The first catcher to wear glasses initially played for the Yankees in 1951 and spent most of his career with Washington. Do you recall him?

10. Against what team did Babe Ruth hit his first home run?

1. *Ernie Banks, Catfish Hunter and Al Kaline.*

2. *Luis Tiant. He struck out 19 Twins in ten innings for Cleveland in 1968.*

3. *Boston Red Sox, Oakland A's, California Angels, Montreal Expos, San Diego Padres and Seattle Mariners.*

4. *Chuck Dressen, 1951-52; Walter Alston, 1953-76; Tommy Lasorda, 1976-present.*

5. *Washington Senators, Kansas City A's and the New York Yankees.*

6. *Fernando Valenzuela and Dwight Gooden.*

7. *Joe Cowley of the White Sox.*

8. *Don Zimmer.*

9. *Clint Courtney.*

10. *The New York Yankees. He hit it on May 6, 1915 at the Polo Grounds for the Boston Red Sox.*

## Relief Pitch

"The umpire has the awesome power
To send a grown man to the shower,
Yet cannot, in the aftermath
Coerce his kids to take a bath."
— *Bob McKenty*

1. Name the five different teams which Billy Martin has managed.

2. Excluding relievers, give two of the first three pitchers to win the Cy Young Award without attaining 20 victories.

3. What two Yankee teammates topped the American League in hitting in 1984?

4. Who is the only player to hit 20 or more pinch hit homers?

5. Only two men have pitched no-hitters in the years in which they won the Cy Young Award. Give one of them.

6. What team, during the 60's, swept a four-game World Series and were swept? Do you recall the opponents?

7. How many outs are there in an inning?

8. The record for stolen bases by a catcher in a season is 36. It was set within the past 20 years by a player who later managed the team he set it with. Who?

9. What is the Major League record for stolen bases in a season? Who holds it?

10. In the first two games of the season, you go 1 for 4 and 2 for 4. What is your batting average?

1. *Minnesota Twins, Detroit Tigers, Texas Rangers, New York Yankees and Oakland A's.*

2. *Sandy Koufax who was 19-5 in 1964; Tom Seaver . . . 19-10 in 1973; Fernando Valenzuela . . . 13-7 in the strike-shortened 1981 season.*

3. *Don Mattingly and Dave Winfield.*

4. *Cliff Johnson with 20.*

5. *Mike Scott in 1986 and Sandy Koufax in 1963 and '65.*

6. *The Los Angeles Dodgers. They swept the Yankees in 1963 and were swept by the Orioles in 1966.*

7. *Usually six.*

8. *John Wathan of the Royals in 1982.*

9. *130 - set by Rickey Henderson of the A's in 1982.*

10. *.375.*

1.  Four Major Leaguers have fathers who played in the 1960 Yankee-Pirate World Series. Name the fathers and the sons.

2.  Who is the oldest man ever to pitch a shutout?

3.  Houston and the New York Mets both entered the National League in 1962. Each team had its first 20 game winner in 1969. Do you recall these two hurlers?

4.  This 17-game winner for the Angels in '86 was the first collegiate player picked in the 1981 National Hockey League player draft. His father, Ted, played in the NHL with the L. A. Kings and Minnesota North Stars. Who is this player?

5.  For what teams did Reggie Jackson play?

6.  Who was the only player to be World Series MVP despite playing on the losing team?

7.  Who holds the shortstop record for most hits in a season?

8.  What two teams went 109-53 in the 1960's?

9.  Who was the first black to play in the American League? For what team? What Major League team did he later manage?

10. Who's the only catcher to win a home run championship?

# Answers

1. Son - Vance Law, father - Vernon; son - Dale Berra, father - Yogi; son - Joel Skinner, father - Bob; son-Dick Schofield, father - Ducky.

2. Satchel Paige of the St. Louis Browns in 1952. He was 46 years, 75 days old.

3. Houston - Larry Dierker who was 20-13. Mets - Tom Seaver who was 25-7.

4. Kirk McCaskill.

5. Kansas City/Oakland A's, Baltimore Orioles, New York Yankees, and California Angels.

6. Bobby Richardson in 1960.

7. Tony Fernandez of Toronto who got 213 in 1986.

8. The 1961 Yankees and the 1969 Orioles.

9. Larry Doby who played for the Cleveland Indians and managed the Chicago White Sox (for 87 games in 1978).

10. Johnny Bench in 1970 and 1972.

## Relief Pitch

"We went the whole game without going to the bathroom." — *Jack Lietz, one of the umpires at the longest game ever played, over eight hours, between Rochester and Pawtucket in 1981*

1. What three men hit more than 40 home runs in a season and had brothers play in the Majors?

2. Who is the only player to pitch more than 100 games in a season?

3. Two pitchers in the last 70 years have won and lost 20 games in the same season. Give one of them.

4. Four Cy Young Award winners have double initials. The most famous is Don Drysdale. Find two of the other three.

5. What free-swinger has struck out more than any other batter?

6. In what year did the Red Sox win their last World Series?

7. What baseball player wrote a book with the title *Screwball*?

8. In 1982, the New York Yankees had three managers. Name two of them.

9. With one man out and a man on first base, a player hits a grounder to the outfield. When the ball is finally thrown in, both runners are standing on third base. The third baseman tags them both. What's the call?

10. For what team did Warren Spahn play his last Major League game?

# 32    Answers

1. *Henry Aaron - Tommie; Joe DiMaggio - Dom and Vince; Richie Allen - Hank and Ron.*

2. *Mike Marshall - 106 games in 1974.*

3. *Wilbur Wood of the White Sox was 24-20 in 1973; Phil Niekro of the Braves was 21-20 in 1979.*

4. *Mike McCormick - in 1967; Mike Marshall - in 1974; and Steve Stone - in 1980.*

5. *Reggie Jackson.*

6. *1918.*

7. *Tug McGraw.*

8. *Bob Lemon managed 14 games; Gene Michael, 86; and Clyde King, 62.*

9. *The player who hit the ball is out.*

10. *San Francisco Giants.*

1.  What father and son have the most combined hits?

2.  Who was the last rookie pitcher to start the seventh game of a World Series?

3.  What man has managed more than 25 years and never won a pennant?

4.  The second batter in the line-up accidentally led off a game and flied out. May he bat again as the next batter?

5.  In 1978, the Yankees and Red Sox had a one game playoff to determine the winner of the American League East. Name the pitcher, batter, and fielder involved in the last out.

6.  Who has more pinch hits than any other player?

7.  In 1976, these two Royals finished one-two in batting in the American League. Who are they? What was controversial about the winner's last at-bat?

8.  What player stole seven bases in two consecutive World Series?

9.  This hurler pitched a perfect game for the Cleveland Indians. In 1983 they traded him to Atlanta for Brett Butler, Brook Jacoby, Rick Behenna and $150,000. The pitcher proceeded to have a combined 10-20 record for the Braves in 1983, '84 and '85 before being released. Who is this pitcher?

10. What player in 1975 stole 38 consecutive bases?

# **33**     **Answers**

1.   *Gus and Buddy Bell who have more than 4000.*

2.   *Joe Magrane of the Cardinals in 1987.*

3.   *Gene Mauch.*

4.   *Yes. In fact, according to the rules, he has to.*

5.   *Carl Yastrzemski popped up a Goose Gossage fast-ball. Graig Nettles caught it in foul territory.*

6.   *Manny Mota - 150.*

7.   *George Brett beat Hal McRae by one point. A lot of people think that Minnesota left fielder, Steve Brye, purposely let Brett's fly ball drop in the eighth inning so that Brett would win.*

8.   *Lou Brock in 1967 and '68.*

9.   *Len Barker.*

10.  *Davey Lopes.*

1. Who are the only two brothers to hit home runs in All-Star competition?

2. One year, three players tied for the World Series MVP Award. Name the team, the year, and the three players.

3. What is the score of a forfeited game?

4. The Cleveland Indians had three 20-game winners in 1951, 1952 and 1956. Name four of these five players.

5. What Cy Young Award winner co-wrote *The Bronx Zoo*?

6. Who is the only pitcher to throw an Opening Day no-hitter?

7. What Hall of Fame pitcher played his entire career with the Yankees?

8. In 1968, this player hit ten home runs in 20 at-bats. Who was this giant of a man?

9. In 1956, losing three games to two to the Yankees, the Dodgers started this pitcher even though he had only started three of his 62 games pitched that year. He responded with a complete game, ten-inning, 1-0 shutout. Name him.

10. Who was the first black man to lead his league in homers?

# 34    Answers

1. *Joe and Vince DiMaggio. Joe did it in 1939; Vince in 1943.*

2. *The 1981 Los Angeles Dodgers. Pedro Guerrero, Steve Yeager, and Ron Cey.*

3. *9-0.*

4. *Bob Feller, '51; Mike Garcia, '51, '52; Early Wynn, '51, '52, '56; Bob Lemon, '52, '56; Herb Score, '56.*

5. *Sparky Lyle.*

6. *Bob Feller in 1940 - Cleveland beat the White Sox, 1-0.*

7. *Whitey Ford.*

8. *Frank Howard.*

9. *Clem Labine.*

10. *Larry Doby who led the American League in 1952.*

1.  The record for most home runs hit by one player in one ball park is 323. The ball park no longer exists. This should give you enough information to figure out the ball player. Can you?

2.  Of the 300 game winners who pitched in this century, who has the worst winning percentage?

3.  Only one pitcher has struck out ten or more batters in a game more than 100 times. Who?

4.  According to Major League rules, what is the penalty when a pitcher delivers the ball to the batter while he is not facing the plate if the bases are loaded at the time?

5.  True or False? When Roger Maris hit 61 home runs in 1961, he hit more home runs on the road than at Yankee Stadium.

6.  Who has stolen the most bases during his career?

7.  Who were the last players to hit .400 in each league?

8.  What Major League team played some of their "home games" in Milwaukee in 1968 and '69?

9.  Who was the last player-manager to win a pennant?

10. What uniform numbers did Willie Mays, Mickey Mantle and Duke Snider wear for most of their careers?

1. *Mel Ott of the New York Giants who hit 323 of his 511 home runs at the Polo Grounds.*

2. *Gaylord Perry. He was 314 and 265 for a winning percentage of .542.*

3. *Nolan Ryan - he has done it more than 160 times.*

4. *It is a balk and each runner may advance one base.*

5. *True - he hit 31 on the road.*

6. *Lou Brock - 938.*

7. *AL - Ted Williams; NL - Bill Terry.*

8. *The Chicago White Sox.*

9. *Lou Boudreau in 1948 with Cleveland.*

10. *Mays - 24; Mantle - 7; Snider - 4.*

## Relief Pitch

"Once I tried to drown myself with a shower nozzle after I gave up a homer in the ninth. I found out you can't."

— *Dan Quisenberry, Kansas City Royals pitcher*

1. In 1986, the Cincinnati Reds had five players on their roster with 2,000 or more career hits. Can you get them all?

2. True or False? A Houston Astro game at the Astrodome was rained out.

3. What St. Louis Cardinal has hit the most home runs in a season?

4. What's the call if a pitcher throws a pitch which bounces and then hits the batter?

5. Name the four Cy Young Award winners who were not born in the United States.

6. Only two players whose last names begin with the letter "A" have hit more than 40 home runs in a season. Who are they?

7. What slugger hit the first home run in the Astrodome?

8. Who hit the first regular-season home run in the Astrodome? Hint: He played for the Phillies, the Cardinals, the Dodgers, the White Sox and the A's.

9. In the famous "Pine Tar Game," who were the batter and pitcher involved in the incident?

10. When the Pine Tar Game was resumed weeks later, the new Yankee center fielder was a former Cy Young Award winner and the second baseman was a future MVP. Give these two players.

1.    Buddy Bell, Dave Concepcion, Dave Parker, Tony
      Perez, and Pete Rose.

2.    True. The game was canceled because the ran came
      down so hard that the streets were flooded and the
      fans couldn't get to the game. This happened in
      1976.

3.    Johnny Mize with 43 in 1940.

4.    The batter is considered hit by the pitch and is
      awarded first base.

5.    Ferguson Jenkins - Canada; Fernando Valenzuela -
      Mexico; Mike Cuellar - Cuba; Willie Hernandez -
      Puerto Rico.

6.    Henry Aaron and Tony Armas.

7.    Mickey Mantle in an exhibition game held between
      the Astros and Yankees on April 9, 1965.

8.    Richie Allen on April 12, 1965.

9.    George Brett of the Royals hit a home run off Goose
      Gossage of the Yankees.

10.   The center fielder was Ron Guidry; the second base-
      man was Don Mattingly.

1. Everyone thinks that the 1919 Chicago "Black Sox" lost the World Series. In reality, they won the seventh game against the Cincinnati Reds. Why does everyone think that they lost?

2. Which pitcher whose last name begins with the letter "B" has won the most games?

3. Two switch-hitters have gotten 230 hits in one season. One did it in the 70's and another in the 80's. Name them.

4. Who has the most World Series hits?

5. Of the 698 players to play for the St. Louis Browns, only one is in the Hall of Fame primarily for what he did as a Brown. Who is this lifetime .340 hitter?

6. True or False? Babe Ruth played one NFL football game.

7. Name the only pitcher with more than ten letters in his last name who has won more than 200 games. Hint: His first name is Freddie.

8. In the 1950's, the San Francisco Giants had first basemen win the Rookie of the Year Awards in consecutive years. Name these two players - both of whom later won MVP Awards.

9. What Pirate once had 198 singles in the same season that Ruth got 60 home runs?

10. Name the three teams which Oakland beat when they won their three consecutive World Series.

1. *Because they did. The 1919 Series was a best five out of nine. Although Chicago won the seventh game, they lost the eighth game to lose the Series 5 games to 3.*

2. *Bert Blyleven.*

3. *Pete Rose in 1973 and Willie Wilson in 1980.*

4. *Yogi Berra with 71.*

5. *George Sisler.*

6. *False.*

7. *Freddie Fitzsimmons who pitched from 1925 to 1943.*

8. *Orlando Cepeda in 1958; Willie McCovey in 1959.*

9. *Lloyd Waner.*

10. *Cincinnati Reds in 1972; New York Mets, 1973; Los Angeles Dodgers, 1974.*

1. Five Hall-of-Famers have averaged more than 30 home runs per season, more than 100 RBI's per season, and have better than .300 batting averages. How many can you get?

2. What third baseman has hit the most American League home runs?

3. True or False? A deaf-mute played in the Major Leagues and got more than 2,000 hits.

4. In 1953, this Hall-of-Famer was traded along with Joe Garagiola and two other players to the Cubs for six players and $150,000. Who is he?

5. In 1967, a Cincinnati teen-aged pitcher struck out over 200 batters. In 1976, he won one of the Reds' four World Series games. Do you remember him?

6. What four catchers have the most lifetime home runs?

7. "A batted ball not swung at, but intentionally met with the bat and tapped slowly within the infield." This is the *Official Baseball Rules* definition of what?

8. When the American League started, there was no New York franchise. In 1903, a team moved to New York. From what city did it come?

9. Who has played the most games at shortstop?

10. What future Manager of the Year lost 24 games as a pitcher for the Mets in 1962?

1. Babe Ruth, Lou Gehrig, Jimmie Foxx, Ted Williams and Henry Aaron.

2. Graig Nettles.

3. True. Dummy Hoy, who played from 1888 to 1902, was a deaf-mute.

4. Ralph Kiner.

5. Gary Nolan.

6. Johnny Bench, Yogi Berra, Carlton Fisk and Gary Carter.

7. A bunt.

8. Baltimore. The previous year, they were known as the Baltimore Orioles.

9. Luis Aparicio, 2581 games.

10. Roger Craig.

1. What World Series team only batted nine players? Can you name them?

2. True or False? Both Mickey Mantle and Willie Mays played shortstop in the Major Leagues.

3. Excluding pitchers, what Rookie of The Year only played 201 Major League games? Hint: He only played for the Cleveland Indians and he played during the 1980's.

4. Who played in seven World Series during the 60's?

5. What pitcher won the most games in his last season?

6. How many times did Babe Ruth hit more than 50 home runs?

7. The 1963 Cardinals had three players get 200 or more hits each. Name one of them.

8. What father and son combination have the most Major League victories?

9. Who is the last rookie manager to win the World Series?

10. On April 30, 1946, Bob Feller no-hit the Yankees 1-0. The center fielder for Cleveland that day was a man who made the Hall of Fame as a pitcher. Who is he?

# **Answers**

1. The 1976 Cincinnati Reds - Tony Perez, Joe Morgan, Dave Concepcion, Pete Rose, Johnny Bench, George Foster, Cesar Geronimo, Ken Griffey and Dan Driessen.

2. True. Mays played two games and Mantle seven.

3. Joe Charboneau - the 1980 winner of the award.

4. Roger Maris. He played for the Yankees 1960 - 1964 and with the Cardinals 1967 - 1968.

5. Sandy Koufax - 27.

6. Four. In 1920, he hit 54; 1921, 59; 1927, 60; 1928, 54.

7. Dick Groat - 201; Curt Flood - 200; Bill White - 200.

8. Dizzy and Steve Trout have won more than 250.

9. Tom Kelly of the 1987 Twins.

10. Bob Lemon. He played 12 games in the outfield that season (and pitched 32 games).

1.  Name the three teams which have appeared in World Series but never won one.

2.  Who was the first Major Leaguer to have his number retired?

3.  Do you recall the first black pitcher to win 20 games in a season?

4.  In 1892, Pud Galvin and Tim Keefe (both 300 game winners at the time) started a game against one another. The next time that 300 game winners faced one another was June 28, 1986 when Cleveland played California. Give these two pitchers.

5.  Only one pitcher has given up more than 50 home runs in a season. Who is this Dutch-born player?

6.  What Major League team during the '70's wore short pants?

7.  What pitcher had a record of 18-1 in 1959?

8.  Who was the first player in this century to hit four home runs in a game?

9.  Name the two teams in the past 50 years to win the World Series even though they had won fewer than 90 regular season games.

10. If you are picked off first base, are you charged with a "caught stealing"?

1. *St. Louis Browns, Milwaukee Brewers and San Diego Padres.*

2. *Lou Gehrig.*

3. *Don Newcombe in 1951.*

4. *Phil Niekro and Don Sutton.*

5. *Bert Blyleven.*

6. *Chicago White Sox.*

7. *Elroy Face of the Pirates.*

8. *Lou Gehrig in 1932.*

9. *Los Angeles Dodgers - 1981; Minnesota Twins - 1987.*

10. *Only if after the pick-off attempt, you try to advance to the next base.*

### Relief Pitch

"Freddie Patek is the only guy in the major leagues who needs a life preserver to go into the whirlpool bath."

> — *Jim Murray, Los Angeles Times, writing about diminutive shortstop Freddie Patek. The 5'5" Patek once said he'd rather be the shortest player in the majors than the tallest player in the minors.*

1.  Since 1955, five pitchers have won 20 games and batted .300 in the same season. Four of these hurlers are in the Hall of Fame. Can you get three out of five of these pitchers?

2.  The Seattle Pilots franchise lasted only one year - 1969. One of their players (who logged 59 games at third, 59 at second and 26 in the outfield) stole 73 bases to lead the league. Four years later, while with Boston, he again led the league. Who is this 15-year veteran?

3.  Who hit the most home runs in one season: Willie Mays, Mickey Mantle or Henry Aaron?

4.  Steve Carlton lost the game in which he struck out 19 batters because he gave up 2 two-run homers to the same batter. Who?

5.  What was the fate of the Seattle Pilots after 1969?

6.  What NL pitcher hit two grand slams in one game?

7.  In the last 50 years, two Phillies have been named MVP. Who are they?

8.  True or False? The first designated hitter was Mickey Mantle.

9.  The 1980 Oakland A's had three pitchers with 20 or more complete games. Name one member of this trio.

10. Three men who won the MVP Award were the first blacks to play for their respective teams. Can you think of them?

1.  *Don Newcombe - in 1955, he went 20-5 and batted .359; Warren Spahn - 1958, 22-11, .333; Don Drysdale - 1965, 23-12, .300; Bob Gibson - 1970, 23-7, .303; Catfish Hunter - 1971, 21-11, .350.*

2.  *Tommy Harper.*

3.  *Mantle with 54 in 1961. Mays had 52 in 1965 and Aaron hit 47 in 1971.*

4.  *Ron Swoboda of the Mets in 1969.*

5.  *They moved to Milwaukee and were rechristened the "Brewers."*

6.  *Tony Cloninger of the Braves. He is the only National Leaguer to hit two in one game.*

7.  *Jim Konstanty in 1950 and Mike Schmidt in 1980, '81 and '86.*

8.  *False. It was Ron Blomberg of the Yankees in 1973.*

9.  *Rick Langford had 28; Mike Norris, 24; and Matt Keough, 20.*

10. *Jackie Robinson - Dodgers; Ernie Banks - Cubs; and Elston Howard - Yankees.*

1. All nine AL starters in the 1934 All-Star Game made it to the Hall of Fame. Name seven of them.

2. One pitcher led the National League in losses in 1977, '78, '79 and '80. Who is this "loser"?

3. What Texas outfielder was MVP?

4. In the seventh game of the 1986 American League Championship Series, the Red Sox were trailing the Angels by three runs in the ninth inning when two men hit two-run homers. Do you recall them?

5. The first player ever to bat for the Twins was a future American League MVP. Who is he?

6. Who is the only four-time winner of the Cy Young Award?

7. Name the three franchises which have won the World Series within the past 50 years and since moved to different cities?

8. Only three third basemen have won more than one batting title. Give this fearsome threesome.

9. What team has the record for starting the season with the most consecutive wins and who was their manager?

10. This man, who set the mark for most hits in a single season, had two sons play in the Majors. Who is he?

1. *Charlie Gehringer, Heinie Manush, Babe Ruth, Lou Gehrig, Jimmie Foxx, Al Simmons, Joe Cronin, Bill Dickey, and Lefty Gomez.*

2. *Phil Niekro.*

3. *Jeff Burroughs in 1974.*

4. *Don Baylor and Dave Henderson.*

5. *Zoilo Versailles.*

6. *Steve Carlton who won in 1972, '77, '80 and '82.*

7. *New York Giants, Brooklyn Dodgers and Milwaukee Braves.*

8. *Bill Madlock, George Brett and Wade Boggs.*

9. *The 1987 Milwaukee Brewers managed by Tom Trebelhorn.*

10. *George Sisler whose sons, Dave and Dick, also made it to the Majors. (Son George Jr. played minor league ball and continues as a baseball executive at that level.)*

1.  Eight of the nine starters on the 1934 National League All-Star team were elected to the Hall of Fame. Can you get half of them?

2.  Three players whose last names begin with "Z" have hit more than 90 career home runs. Give two of them.

3.  What team played its home games in Jarry Park?

4.  What Major League team's address is 9449 Friars Road?

5.  Name the four teams managed by Leo Durocher.

6.  Only once in the past 60 years have the AL and NL home run champions finished with the same number of homers - they both hit 49. Who are they?

7.  What was the name of the Robert Redford movie in which he played a Major League baseball player?

8.  Two men have hit over 300 home runs and stolen over 300 bases. Who? (Hint: They played in the same outfield for four years.)

9.  Who is the oldest man to hit 40 home runs in a season?

10. With the bases loaded, one out and a full count, you swing and miss at the next pitch - but the ball hits you. What's the call?

# 43    Answers

1. *Frankie Frisch, Pie Traynor, Joe Medwick, Kiki Cuyler, Bill Terry, Travis Jackson, Gabby Hartnett and Carl Hubbell. Wally Berger of the Braves was the only starter not elected to the Hall.*

2. *Gus Zernial - 237; Richie Zisk - 207; Don Zimmer - 91.*

3. *Montreal Expos.*

4. *The San Diego Padres (Jack Murphy Stadium).*

5. *Brooklyn Dodgers, New York Giants, Chicago Cubs and Houston Astros.*

6. *In 1987, Andre Dawson of the Cubs and Mark McGwire of the A's each led his league with 49.*

7. *The Natural.*

8. *Willie Mays - 660 HR, 338 SB; Bobby Bonds - 332 HR, 461 SB.*

9. *Darrell Evans.*

10. *You're out! Runners advance at their own risk; the ball is not dead.*

1. Only two Hispanic players have hit more than 45 home runs in a season. Who?

2. In 1974, this catcher/first baseman led the AL in walks; three years later he led the NL in free passes. In both these years, he had more walks than hits. Who is this former World Series MVP?

3. What team plays its home games in a stadium named for a former Vice President of the United States?

4. What player holds the record for the longest consecutive-game hitting streak for a catcher?

5. Two Cy Young winners have ten letters in their last names. Can you get at least one of them?

6. This infielder, who played from 1967 to 1983, has five different vowels in his first name and four different vowels in his surname. Name him.

7. In 1981, Rollie Fingers won the Cy Young Award. What team did he play with that year? What club did he play with in 1980? What other team came in-between?

8. Who was the first black to win a batting title?

9. What speedster led the American League in stolen bases every year from 1956 to 1964?

10. From 1960 to 1982, 25 All-Star Games were played. How many did the AL win?

1.  Orlando Cepeda with 46 in 1961 and George Bell who clouted 47 in 1987.

2.  Gene Tenace.

3.  The Twins who play in the Hubert H. Humphrey Metrodome.

4.  Benito Santiago who hit safely in 34 straight games in 1987.

5.  Fernando Valenzuela and Bret Saberhagen.

6.  Aurelio Rodriguez.

7.  On December 8, 1980, San Diego traded Fingers to St. Louis. Four days later, the Cards dealt him to Milwaukee where he won the Award.

8.  Jackie Robinson in 1949.

9.  Luis Aparicio.

10. Two - in 1962 and 1971.

1. Who holds the record for most stolen bases in a season by an infielder?

2. In 1920, Babe Ruth led the Majors in home runs with 54. Within five, how many homers did the runner-up have?

3. A member of the 1960 World Champion Pirates is the only pitcher to have lost 200 or more games without winning at least 200. Do you remember him?

4. What catcher, who played during the 70's and 80's, has caught the most games in Major League history?

5. Give the first three lefthanded winners of the Cy Young Award.

6. In 1962, a Boston Red Sox hurler became the first black man to throw a no-hitter in the American League. Who is he?

7. Who is the only AL pitcher to win 20 games with a last place club?

8. What fifteen-year veteran counted "Calvin Coolidge Julius Caesar Tuskahoma" among his given names?

9. There have been five catchers to receive the Rookie-of-the-Year Award. Can you get four of them?

10. Who led the National League in stolen bases four consecutive years during the 50's?

1.   *Maury Wills with 104 in 1962.*

2.   *19 - by George Sisler.*

3.   *Bob Friend with a career record of 197-230.*

4.   *Bob Boone.*

5.   *Warren Spahn - 1957; Whitey Ford - 1961; Sandy Koufax - 1963.*

6.   *Earl Wilson.*

7.   *Nolan Ryan in 1974 with California when he was 22-16.*

8.   *Cal McLish.*

9.   *Johnny Bench - 1968; Thurman Munson - 1970; Earl Williams - 1971; Carlton Fisk - 1972; Benito Santiago - 1987.*

10.   *Willie Mays.*

## Relief Pitch

"Well, I see in the game in Minnesota that Terry Felton has relieved himself on the mound in the second inning."

> — *Royals announcer Fred White, upon noticing a typographical error indicating that Twins pitcher Terry Felton started the game and also came on in relief*

1. In the 1987 National League Championship, Todd Worrell pitched and played another position in the same game. Only one player has ever done this in a World Series game. Who?

2. What pitcher, who pitched during the 60's, led the league in wins, strike outs and lowest E.R.A. in the same season on three different occasions?

3. Who holds the record for most career doubles?

4. Who holds the Toronto Blue Jay record for most career home runs?

5. Who is the only man to hit more than 40 home runs in a season and later have a son play in the Majors. (Hint: In 1936, he hit 42 home runs and knocked in 162 runs with Cleveland.)

6. Name the three players on the '73 Braves who hit 40 home runs apiece.

7. What Dodger pitcher won two games and saved two during the 1959 Series?

8. Name one of the two players to have won 16 Gold Glove Awards.

9. What player who once hit safely in 30 straight games also led each league in stolen bases - once with Montreal and once with Detroit?

10. Who stole home the most times?

1.    *Babe Ruth. In game 4 of the 1918 World Series, he pitched the first eight innings and moved to left field for the ninth inning. Ruth won the game 3 to 2.*

2.    *Sandy Koufax in 1963, '65, and '66.*

3.    *Tris Speaker with 793.*

4.    *Jessie Barfield.*

5.    *Hal Trosky whose son was also Hal Trosky.*

6.    *Davey Johnson - 43; Darrell Evans - 41; Hank Aaron - 40.*

7.    *Larry Sherry. For this performance, he was voted World Series MVP.*

8.    *Brooks Robinson for third base and Jim Kaat for pitcher.*

9.    *Ron LeFlore.*

10.   *Ty Cobb.*

1. This National League MVP finished second in the nation in scoring in college basketball during the 1951-52 season. Who?

2. What first baseman, on a pennant-winning team during the 1980's, did not hit a single home run even though he got up 493 times?

3. Name one of the three players to hit four home runs in a game during the 1950's.

4. Who is the last player to hit four home runs in a game?

5. What Hall-of-Famer's first and middle names are Denton True?

6. In what town was the game played in the poem, *Casey at the Bat?*

7. What National League pitcher led the league in victories for five consecutive seasons from 1957-1961?

8. The 1937 Tigers had four 200-hit players. Name one of them.

9. What three pitchers hold the Major League record for best season strikeout ratio?

10. What rookie has knocked in the most runs in a season?

1.    *Dick Groat who played for Duke.*

2.    *Pete Rose of the 1983 Phillies.*

3.    *Gil Hodges - 1950; Joe Adcock - 1954; and Rocky Colavito - 1959.*

4.    *Bob Horner of the Braves.*

5.    *Cy Young.*

6.    *Mudville.*

7.    *Warren Spahn - he won 21 four times and 22 the other time.*

8.    *Gee Walker - 213; Charlie Gehringer - 209; Pete Fox - 208; Hank Greenberg - 200. The Tigers finished in second place, 13 games behind the Yankees.*

9.    *Nolan Ryan - 11.48 K's per 9 innings, 1987; Dwight Gooden - 11.39, 1984; and Sam McDowell - 10.71, 1965. Ryan was 40 years old when he set this record.*

10.   *Ted Williams - 145 in 1939.*

1.  Name five of the seven AL players whose last names begin with "B" and who have won the MVP Award within the past 50 years.

2.  Where is the Little League World Series held each year?

3.  Who had the most home runs by his 25th birthday? (Hint: He was a member of the 1968 World Champion Tigers.)

4.  Which single-digit uniform numbers have not been retired by the Yankees?

5.  What team has won ten post-season games in one year?

6.  Where is the National Baseball Hall of Fame located?

7.  What player led the NL in triples with Atlanta and the AL while with Cleveland?

8.  Name the two players who have won the Triple Crown twice.

9.  The 1967 Chicago White Sox won 89 games and finished only three games out of first place despite a team batting average of .225. They did have three of the AL's top four E.R.A. leaders. Do you recall at least one member of this trio?

10. What pitcher twice led the National League in E.R.A. and strikeouts in the same season but failed to win the Cy Young either year?

1. Lou Boudreau, 1948; Yogi Berra, 1951, '54, '55; Jeff Burroughs, 1974; Don Baylor, 1979; George Brett, 1980; George Bell, 1987; and, the only pitcher, Vida Blue, 1971.

2. Williamsport, Pennsylvania.

3. Ed Mathews.

4. 2 and 6.

5. The 1981 Los Angeles Dodgers. They won three against Houston to win the West, three against Montreal for the pennant, and four over the Yankees in the Series.

6. Cooperstown, New York.

7. Brett Butler. He did it with the Braves in 1983 and with the Indians in 1980.

8. Ted Williams in 1941 and '47; Rogers Hornsby who did it in 1922 and '25.

9. Joel Horlen - 2.06; Gary Peters - 2.28; Tommy John - 2.47. Sonny Siebert of the Indians finished in third place with a 2.38 E.R.A.

10. Tom Seaver in 1970 and '71. In 1970, he lost out to Bob Gibson; in 1971, he was topped in the voting by Ferguson Jenkins. Seaver did win the Cy Young Award in 1969 and '73.

1. List four of the six switch-hitters to hit 30 or more home runs in a season.

2. Within three, what is the single-season record for homers hit in one stadium?

3. What 300 game winner did not even have 200 victories by his 40th birthday?

4. It has happened four times in National League history that a play-off has been required to break a tie between two teams at the end of the scheduled season. One club has been involved in all four such tie-breakers. Name this team and its four opponents.

5. What's the call? First and third, one out. The batter hits a long fly to deep right field which is caught. The runner on third tags up and scores. The runner on first, thinking that the ball would drop, is almost to third base before he realizes that the catch has been made. He re-traces his steps but the throw beats him to complete the double play. Does the run count?

6. Four players have hit World Series home runs in 1-0 games. Name one of these men.

7. What are Babe Ruth's first and middle names?

8. Who is Masonori Murakami?

9. Can you give the three American Leaguers who have hit two grand slams in a game?

10. Who has the best NL season batting average in the past 30 years?

1. *Mickey Mantle, Reggie Smith, Ken Singleton, Eddie Murray, Howard Johnson, and Ripper Collins.*

2. *39 by Hank Greenberg of the Tigers.*

3. *Phil Niekro.*

4. *The Dodgers have been involved in all four play-offs. The Brooklyn Dodgers lost to the Cardinals in 1946 and the Giants in 1951. The Los Angeles Dodgers beat the Braves in 1959 and lost to the Giants in 1962.*

5. *There are three outs but the run scores. (This assumes that the runner on third touched home before the final out was made.)*

6. *Casey Stengel in 1923; Tommy Henrich in 1949; Paul Blair and Frank Robinson in 1966.*

7. *George Herman.*

8. *The Japanese player who pitched with the San Francisco Giants in 1964-65. He was 5-1 in 54 games.*

9. *Frank Robinson, Jim Northrup and Jim Gentile.*

10. *Tony Gwynn of the Padres in 1987. He batted .370.*

1. Only three players have hit more than 300 home runs and 150 triples. Can you think of two of them?

2. This NL MVP's brother finished second to Jesse Owens in the 200 meter run in the 1936 Olympics. Name him and his brother.

3. At the end of three innings, the visiting pitcher has faced only nine batters. No one has been up out of order. What is the most pitches that the clean-up batter could have faced if he didn't foul off any pitches?

4. What first baseman, who was not known as a good fielder, played 159 games without making an error in 1984?

5. In 1985, these two Cardinals combined for 166 stolen bases. Who are they?

6. Three shortstops have accumulated more than 200 hits, 100 RBI's, 100 runs scored and 20 home runs - and they hit better than .300 in the same season. Name them.

7. Why were Lou Gehrig and Babe Ruth assigned uniform numbers 3 and 4, respectively?

8. What Hispanic pitcher has struck out the most batters in a season?

9. Who was baseball's first Commissioner?

10. Cookie Lavagetto had two World Series hits in 17 at-bats. Both occurred with two outs in the ninth inning of a game that the Dodgers won 3-2. He got the first hit in the 1941 Series and the second in 1947. Name the two pitchers off whom he got these hits. (Hint: One of these pitchers has the exact same name as the author of this book.)

1. *Lou Gehrig - 493 home runs, 162 triples; Stan Musial - 475, 177; Rogers Hornsby - 301, 169. Willie Mays "only" had 140 triples.*

2. *Jackie Robinson. His brother, Matthew "Mack" Robinson, won the silver medal.*

3. *The answer is eleven. One way that it can happen is as follows: He gets up in the first inning with a man on first and two outs. The count goes to three and two. The pitcher then picks off the runner for the third out. When the clean-up hitter leads off the second inning, he walks on a 3-2 pitch.*

4. *Steve Garvey.*

5. *Vince Coleman - 110 and Willie McGee - 56.*

6. *Robin Yount - 1982; Cal Ripkin, Jr. - 1983; and Alan Trammell - 1987.*

7. *Because that was their usual spot in the batting order.*

8. *Luis Tiant of Cuba who struck out 264 in 1968.*

9. *Kenesaw "Mountain" Landis.*

10. *He got his first hit off John Murphy of the Yankees. His second hit, the famous one, was a two-out double off Bill Bevens of the Yanks. This hit broke up a no-hitter and turned a 2-1 deficit into a victory.*

# The
# Bathroom Library

THE BATHROOM SPORTS QUIZ BOOK
THE BATHROOM ENTERTAINMENT BOOK
THE BATHROOM TRIVIA BOOK
THE BATHROOM DIGEST
THE BATHROOM CROSSWORD
  PUZZLE BOOK
THE BATHROOM GUEST BOOK
THE BATHROOM GAME BOOK
THE BATHROOM INSPIRATION BOOK
THE BATHROOM BASEBALL BOOK

For further information, write to:
Red-Letter Press, Inc.
P.O. Box 393,
Saddle River, N.J. 07458